pasta
perfect

TRIDENT PRESS INTERNATIONAL

Published by:
TRIDENT PRESS INTERNATIONAL
801 12th Avenue South
Suite 302
Naples, FL 34102 U.S.A.
(c)Trident Press
Tel: (941) 649 7077
Fax: (941) 649 5832
Email: tridentpress@worldnet.att.net
Website: www.trident-international.com

acknowledgements

Pasta perfect
Packaged by R&R Publications Marketing Pty Ltd
Creative Director: Paul Sims
Production Manager: Paul Sims
Food Photography: Warren Webb, Andrew Elton, Quentin Bacon, Gary Smith, Per Ericson, Paul Grater, Ray Joice, John Stuart, Ashley Mackevicius, Harm Mol, Yanto Noerianto, Andy Payne.
Food Stylists: Stephanie Souvlis, Janet Lodge, Di Kirby, Wendy Berecry, Belinda Clayton, Rosemary De Santis, Carolyn Fienberg, Jacqui Hing, Michelle Gorry, Christine Sheppard, Donna Hay
Recipe Development: Ellen Argyriou, Sheryle Eastwood, Kim Freeman, Lucy Kelly, Donna Hay, Anneka Mitchell, Penelope Peel, Jody Vassallo, Belinda Warn, Loukie Werle.
Proof Reader: Samantha Calcott

All rights reserved. No part of this book
may be stored, reproduced or transmitted
in any form or by any means without written
permission of the publisher, except in the
case of brief quotations embodied in
critical articles and reviews.

Includes Index
ISBN 1 582 79111 2
EAN 9 781582 791111

First Edition Printed September 2000
Computer Typeset in Humanist 521
& Times New Roman

Printed by APP Printing, Singapore
Film Scanning by PICA Overseas, Singapore

contents

Introduction
4

Starters
6

Meat & poultry
18

Seafood
40

Vegetables
54

Types of pasta
74

Techniques
76

Weights & measures
78

Index
80

introduction

Pasta in all its forms has graced tables in Italy and indeed all over the globe for thousands of years. Recognised as one of the world's most beloved foods, pasta possesses qualities that quite possibly will make it the 21st century's food of choice. Pasta's superior nutritional benefits have earned it superfood status. It is also the ideal staple; economical, convenient to store and prepare, it is versatile and highly pleasurable to eat. In fact one could quite easily call pasta "the perfect food".

Pasta Fresh and Dried:

Pasta is made from grain combined with liquid (and sometimes with other ingredients for flavouring and colouring). Kneading produces a smooth dough or paste (hence the word pasta), that can be rolled out or cut and formed into any of hundreds of varieties. Making sense out of the multitude of pasta varieties is simplified by dividing pasta into two categories: fresh and dried.

Basic ingredients:

The basic ingredients of fresh pasta are flour and eggs, with perhaps a little oil or water added to make the dough easier to work, with some salt for flavour.

Most commercially produced dried pasta is made from water and semolina, a special variety of flour ground from high quality durum wheat.

Semolina creates a firm, elastic dough that is sturdy enough to be shaped by a machine. It can also be used in homemade pasta, either alone or mixed with all-purpose flour, to strengthen the dough and enhance the texture of the finished product.

Nutritional value

Pasta is valued as a high-energy, low-fat food, and a high source of dietary fibre. It supplies moderate amounts of protein and some of the B group vitamins, especially thiamine. The sauces and their ingredients served with pasta will increase the nutritive content. With an informed choice, fat content can remain low, making pasta meals ideal for healthy eating.

How to cook value

You need to follow only a few well-trodden rules to achieve perfect pasta every time. If you adhere to the following steps you will never produce pasta that is soggy or sticky.

Use a big pan and lots of water. As the Italian's love to say, "pasta loves to swim".

Let the water come to full boiling point before adding salt.

With the water boiling freely add the pasta a few handfuls at a time and stir gently to stop it sticking together.

Cover the pan to allow the water to return to the boil quickly, but watch to ensure that the pot does not boil over. When foam rises to the top of the pan lower the heat to maintain a soft boil.

Test pasta by biting into a selected strand. The pasta is done when it tastes good, with just that little bit of firmness. It should be deliciously chewy without a floury taste, what the Italian's call "al dente", which means "just right to the tooth".

Different thicknesses of dried pasta require different cooking times. It should also be noted that fresh pasta, with its higher moisture content, will usually cook much more quickly than even the thinnest dried pasta. When cooked immediately drain the pasta. Do not rinse it, unless the directions specifically say so as washing will reduce the nutrients in the meal.

Always sauce the pasta at once, to keep it from sticking, tossing well to distribute the sauce evenly.

Pasta that is to be sauced and baked, should be undercooked slightly: otherwise it will be too soft after baking.

With spaghetti, apply a light sauce to a fine stick, such as angel-hair, and a more robust sauce to a thicker strand. A rule of thumb, therefore, would be to ensure that the sauce grades increase with the thickness of the spaghetti, linguine or fettuccine used.

When using tubular pasta try a clinging sauce that will stick to them both inside and out, whilst shell shaped pasta is shaped just right for holding puddles of sauce and pieces of meat, fish or poultry.

Twists are more versatile as they will allow a robust sauce to wrap around them for a full-flavour dish, or they can accept a light vinaigrette when served in a cold salad.

Sauce ingredients are only limited by the cook's imagination and desire to experiment. We have included a number of very tasty sauces throughout this book, however we would encourage you to experiment and experience the delight of creating your own marvellous dish, using your favourite pasta as a base.

The best oils for pasta

The subtle flavour of pasta is enhanced by good-quality olive oil. The flavour and quality of olive oil varies according to the type of olives it was pressed from, where the olives were grown and the method of pressing. Olive oils are graded according to how much oleic acid they contain and the procedure used to make them. The oil must be pressed from olives that were not chemically treated in order to qualify for one of the following top four categories:

- Virgin (no more than 4 percent oleic acid)
- Fine virgin (no more than 3 percent oleic acid)
- Superfine virgin (no more than 2 percent oleic acid)
- Extra virgin (no more than 1 percent oleic acid)

Storing and using olive oil

- Choose olive oil with a clean, fruity aroma, full body, and fruity or peppery flavour
- Store olive oil where it will not be exposed to heat or light, which can cause it to become rancid. Use within a years time.
- Use a good-tasting affordable olive oil for sautéed and baked disks; save the finest grades for pesto and other uncooked dishes or for drizzling over cooked foods just before serving.

starters

Campellini with tomatoes

Healthy soups are made hearty by the addition

of pasta; add it to vegetables, meat and vegetable or chicken soups.

Vermicelli is a fine-strand pasta, suitable for inclusion in broths or puréed soups (first break the strands into 5cm/2in pieces). Elbows, spirals, trivelle and rigatoni are more suitable for big "chunky" soups.

What better choice for an entrée than pasta with a delicious sauce to stimulate the appetite. Fettuccine is perhaps the most popular choice and will go well when matched with a variety of sauces. You will find a very tasty of sauces to make within this chapter.

Like many other dishes based on pasta, soups and salads offer creative, delicious opportunities for using up leftover shellfish, poultry, meats or vegetables.

A moderate serving of lasagne or stuffed cannelloni are also popular entrée choices, although we have included recipes for these in other chapters of this book.

capellini
with tomatoes

Photograph Page 7

Method:

1. *Heat 60mL/2oz of the oil in a pan, add the garlic, and cook over a medium heat (until the garlic is slightly browned and golden).*
2. *Reduce the heat, and add the tomatoes, basil, salt and pepper, and cook for 5 minutes (or until tomatoes are just heated through).*
3. *Cook cappellini pasta in boiling salted water (until al dente). Add remaining oil.*
4. *Serve with tomato mixture over cappellini pasta.*

Serves 4-6

ingredients

120mL/4 fl oz olive oil
6 cloves garlic, thinly sliced
550g/17oz Roma tomatoes, seeded and diced
1/3 cup fresh basil, shredded
salt
freshly ground black pepper
400g/13oz cappellini

---

spaghetti
basil soup

Photograph Page 9

Method:

1. *Cook spaghetti in boiling water in a large saucepan following packet directions. Drain and set aside.*
2. *Heat oil in a large saucepan and cook onion, garlic and almonds, stirring over a medium heat for 6-7 minutes or until onions are transparent.*
3. *Add stock and basil to pan and bring to the boil, reduce heat, cover and simmer for 10 minutes. Stir in spaghetti and season to taste with black pepper. Spoon soup into bowls and serve immediately.*

Serves 4

ingredients

155g/5oz spaghetti, broken into pieces
2 tablespoons vegetable oil
1 onion, chopped
2 cloves garlic, crushed
60g/2oz slivered almonds
4 cups/1L/1 3/4pt chicken stock
30g/1oz fresh basil leaves, shredded
freshly ground black pepper

caviar fettuccine

Method:

1. Cook fettuccine in boiling water in a large saucepan, following packet directions. Drain, set aside and keep warm.
2. Heat oil in a large frying pan and cook garlic over low heat for 3-4 minutes. Add fettuccine, chives, red and black caviar, and eggs to pan. Toss to combine. Serve immediately, topped with sour cream.

Serves 4

ingredients

- 300g/9½oz fettuccine
- 2 tablespoons olive oil
- 2 cloves garlic, crushed
- 2 tablespoons finely snipped fresh chives
- 3 tablespoons red caviar
- 3 tablespoons black caviar
- 2 hard-boiled eggs, chopped
- 4 tablespoons sour cream

fettuccine
with coriander (cilantro) sauce

Method:

1 Cook fettuccine in boiling water in a large saucepan following packet directions. Drain, set aside and keep warm.
2 To make sauce, place garlic, walnuts, coriander (cilantro) and parsley in a food processor or blender and process to finely chop. With machine running, add oil in a steady stream. Add Parmesan cheese and black pepper to taste, and process to combine.
3 Spoon sauce over pasta and toss to combine. Serve immediately.

Serves 6

ingredients

500g/1 lb fettuccine
Coriander (cilantro) sauce
2 cloves garlic, chopped
60g/2oz walnut pieces
60g/2oz coriander (cilantro) leaves
15g/¹/₂oz fresh parsley leaves
4 tablespoons vegetable oil
60g/2oz grated Parmesan cheese
freshly ground black pepper

tomato pasta rolls

ingredients

2 cups/250g/8oz flour
2 eggs
2 tablespoons water
2 tablespoons concentrated tomato paste (purée)
1 tablespoon olive oil

<u>Spinach filling</u>
500g/1 lb frozen spinach, thawed and well drained
375g/12oz ricotta or cottage cheese
2 eggs
90g/3oz grated Parmesan cheese
1 teaspoon ground nutmeg
freshly ground black pepper
12 slices prosciutto or thinly sliced ham
500g/1 lb sliced mozzarella cheese

Method:

1. Place flour, eggs, water, tomato paste (purée) and oil in a food processor and process to combine. Turn dough onto a lightly floured surface and knead for 5 minutes or until it is smooth and elastic. Wrap dough in plastic food wrap and set aside to stand for 15 minutes.

2. To make filling, place spinach, ricotta or cottage cheese, eggs, Parmesan cheese, nutmeg and black pepper (to taste) in a bowl, and mix to combine.

3. Divide dough in two halves and roll out one half to form a rectangle 30x45cm/12x18in. Spread with half the filling mixture, leaving a 2.5cm/1in border, then top with half the prosciutto or ham and half the mozzarella cheese. Fold in borders on long sides, then roll up from the short side. Wrap roll in a piece of washed calico cloth and secure ends with string. Repeat with remaining ingredients to make a second roll.

4. Half fill a baking dish with water and place on the stove top. Bring to the boil, add rolls, reduce heat, cover dish with aluminium foil or lid and simmer for 30 minutes. Turn rolls once or twice during cooking. Remove rolls from water and allow to cool for 5 minutes. Remove calico from rolls and refrigerate until firm. To serve, cut rolls into slices.

Serves 12

spaghetti
and pesto

Method:

1. Cook spaghetti in boiling water in a large saucepan following packet directions. Drain, set aside and keep warm.
2. To make Pesto, place basil, pine nuts and garlic in a food processor or blender and process to finely chop all ingredients. With machine running, add oil in a steady steam. Season to taste with black pepper.
3. Add Pesto to spaghetti and toss to combine. Serve immediately.

Serves 6

ingredients

500g/1 lb spaghetti
<u>Pesto</u>
125g/4oz fresh basil leaves
3 tablespoons pine nuts
4 cloves garlic, crushed
4 tablespoons olive oil
freshly ground black pepper

chicken & leek rolls

Method:

1. Cook lasagne sheets in boiling water in a large saucepan until tender. Drain, set aside and keep warm.
2. To make filling, heat oil in a large frying pan and cook leeks and chicken, stirring, for 4-5 minutes or until chicken is brown. Stir in stock, cornflour mixture, mustard and basil and cook, stirring, for 2 minutes longer. Season to taste with black pepper.
3. Place spoonfuls of filling on lasagne sheets, roll up, top with Parmesan cheese and serve immediately.

Serves 6

ingredients

12 spinach lasagne sheets
<u>Chicken and leek filling</u>
2 teaspoons vegetable oil
3 leeks, finely sliced
3 chicken breast fillets, cut into thin strips
$^1/_2$ cup/125mL/4 fl oz chicken stock
3 teaspoons cornflour blended with 2 tablespoons water
1 teaspoon French mustard
2 teaspoons chopped fresh basil
freshly ground black pepper
2 tablespoons grated fresh Parmesan cheese, for garnish

minestrone

Method:
1. Place dried beans and 4 cups/1L/1¾ pt water in a large bowl, cover and set aside to soak for 8 hours or overnight.
2. Drain beans and rinse in cold water. Place beans and stock in a large saucepan, bring to the boil and boil for 10 minutes, then reduce heat, cover and simmer for 1 hour or until beans are tender.
3. Add mushrooms, green beans, carrots, zucchini (courgettes), leek and remaining water to pan. Bring to the boil, then reduce heat, cover and simmer for 30 minutes. Stir pasta and tomatoes into soup and cook for 10 minutes longer or until pasta is tender. Season to taste with black pepper. Sprinkle with Parmesan cheese and serve immediately.

Serves 6

ingredients

315g/10oz dried white beans
6 cups/1.5L/2½pt water
6 cups/1.5L/2½pt chicken stock
125g/4oz mushrooms, sliced
155g/5oz green beans, chopped
2 carrots, chopped
2 zucchini (courgettes), sliced
1 leek, sliced
155g/5oz small shell pasta
440g/14oz canned tomatoes, undrained and mashed
freshly ground black pepper
grated Parmesan cheese

noodles
with bok choy sauce

Method:
1. Cook noodles in boiling water in a large saucepan, following packet directions. Drain, set aside and keep warm.
2. To make sauce, heat oil in a wok or frying pan over a high heat, add bok choy and stir-fry for 2-3 minutes. Add soy sauce, sesame oil, kechap manis, chilli sauce and ginger. Bring to a simmer and cook for 1 minute.
3. Add tofu and bean sprouts and stir-fry for 2-3 minutes or until heated through. Add noodles to pan and toss to combine. Serve immediately.

Serves 4

ingredients

250g/8oz quick-cooking noodles
Bok choy sauce
1 tablespoon vegetable oil
2 bunches/500g/1 lb baby bok choy, leaves separated and trimmed
1/3 cup/90mL/3 fl oz soy sauce
2 tablespoons sesame oil
2 tablespoons kechap manis
2 tablespoons sweet chilli sauce
2 tablespoons pickled ginger
315g/10oz tofu, cut into 1 cm/1/2in cubes
15g/5oz bean sprouts

crispy noodles
and vegetables

Method:
1. Cook noodles in boiling water in a large saucepan for 2-3 minutes, drain and dry on absorbent kitchen paper. Heat oil in a large saucepan over a medium heat until a cube of bread dropped in browns in 50 seconds. Deep-fry noodles, in batches, for 2-3 minutes or until puffed and crispy. Drain on absorbent kitchen paper, set aside and keep warm.
2. Cook mixed vegetables following packet directions. Drain, set aside and keep warm.
3. To make sauce, place peanut butter, sugar, garlic, coconut milk, soy sauce and chilli sauce in a saucepan and cook over a low heat, stirring, for 3-5 minutes or until hot. To serve, divide noodles between serving plates, top with vegetables and sauce.

Serves 4

ingredients

315g/10oz fresh thin egg noodles
vegetable oil for deep-frying
500g/1 lb packaged frozen Chinese stir-fry mixed vegetables
Peanut sauce
3/4 cup/200g/6 1/2oz crunchy peanut butter
1 tablespoon brown sugar
1 clove garlic, crushed
1 1/2 cups/375mL/12 fl oz coconut milk
2 tablespoons light soy sauce
2 teaspoons hot chilli sauce

Ravioli and vegetable medley

meat & poultry

For nutritious and filling main meals,

pasta served with a substantial sauce of meat or poultry is the answer.

For one-pot pasta dinners, braise cubes of meat or chicken pieces with onion and garlic for 30 minutes, then add 220g/7oz shell pasta or pasta spirals, 2 tablespoons tomato paste and enough hot water to cover. Continue to simmer for a further 25 minutes and the meal is ready. Serve with a sprinkling of grated Romano or Parmesan cheese.

penne
bacon & basil

ingredients

500g/1 lb penne
1 tablespoon olive oil
2 cloves garlic, crushed
6 rashers bacon, chopped
2 tablespoons chopped fresh basil
60g/2oz chopped walnuts
freshly ground black pepper
30g/1oz grated Parmesan cheese

Method:

1 Cook penne in boiling water in a large saucepan, following packet directions. Drain, set aside and keep warm.

2 Heat oil in a large frying pan and cook garlic over a medium heat for 1 minute. Add bacon and cook for 2-3 minutes longer or until bacon is crispy. Add basil, walnuts and penne to pan, season to taste with black pepper and toss to combine. Sprinkle with Parmesan cheese and serve immediately.

Serves 4

ravioli
with vegetable medley

Photograph Page 19

ingredients

500g/1 lb ravioli of your choice
30g/1oz butter
2 cloves garlic, crushed
125g/4oz button mushrooms, halved
125g/4oz green beans, cut into 1cm/^{1}/$_2$in lengths
125g/4oz cherry tomatoes, quartered
freshly ground black pepper
30g/1oz grated Parmesan cheese

Method:

1 Cook ravioli in boiling water in a large saucepan, following packet directions. Drain, set aside and keep warm.

2 Melt butter in a large frying pan and cook garlic and mushrooms for 2-3 minutes. Add beans and tomatoes, season to taste with black pepper and cook for 2 minutes longer.

3 Add ravioli and Parmesan cheese to pan and toss to combine. Serve immediately.

Serves 4

fettuccine
with leeks

Method:

1. Cook fettuccine in boiling water in a large saucepan following packet directions. Drain, set aside and keep warm.
2. Heat butter in a large frying pan and cook leeks for 8-10 minutes or until tender. Add ham and red capsicum (pepper) and cook for 2-3 minutes longer. Stir in cream, bring to the boil, then reduce heat and simmer for 4-5 minutes.
3. Add fettuccine to pan and toss to combine. Season with black pepper (to taste) and serve immediately.

Serves 4

ingredients

500g/1 lb fettuccine
60g/2oz butter
2 large leeks, halved and thinly sliced
185g/6oz ham, cut into strips
1 red capsicum (pepper), cut into strips
1 cup/250mL/8 fl oz thickened (double) cream
freshly ground black pepper

cheesy meatballs & spaghetti

Method:

1 *To make meatballs, place beef, parsley, Parmesan cheese, tomato paste (purée) and egg in a bowl, and mix to combine. Form mixture into small balls and cook in a non-stick frying pan for 4-5 minutes or until brown. Remove meatballs from pan and drain on absorbent kitchen paper.*

2 *To make sauce, melt butter in a large frying pan and cook onion, basil and oregano for 2-3 minutes or until onion is soft. Stir in tomatoes, tomato paste (purée), beef stock, wine and sugar. Bring to the boil, then reduce heat and simmer, stirring occasionally, for 30 minutes or until sauce reduces and thickens. Season to taste with black pepper. Add meatballs to sauce and cook for 5 minutes longer.*

3 *Cook spaghetti in boiling water in a large saucepan following packet directions. Drain, place in a warm serving bowl and top with meatballs and sauce. Serve immediately.*

What's the easiest way to eat ribbon pasta?

Firstly, serve it in a shallow bowl or on a plate with a slight rim. To ensure that the pasta stays hot while you are eating it, heat the plates before serving. To eat the pasta, slip a few strands on to your fork, then twirl them against the plate, or a spoon, into a ball – the trick is to take only small forkfuls and to wind the pasta tightly so that there are no dangling strands.

Serves 4

ingredients

250g/8oz spaghetti
<u>**Cheesy meatballs**</u>
500g/1 lb lean beef mince
2 tablespoons finely chopped fresh parsley
½ cup/60g/2oz grated Parmesan cheese
2 teaspoons tomato paste (purée)
1 egg, beaten
<u>**Tomato sauce**</u>
15g/½oz butter
1 onion, finely chopped
2 teaspoons dried basil
1 teaspoon dried oregano
440g/14oz canned tomatoes, undrained and mashed
2 tablespoons tomato paste (purée)
½ cup/125mL/4 fl oz beef stock
½ cup/125mL/4 fl oz white wine
1 teaspoon caster sugar
freshly ground black pepper

fettuccine
carbonara

Method:

1 Cook pasta in boiling water in a large saucepan following packet directions. Drain, set aside and keep warm.
2 To make sauce, cook ham, prosciutto or bacon in a frying pan over a medium heat for 3 minutes or until crisp.
3 Stir in stock and cream, bring to simmering and simmer until sauce is reduced by half.
4 Remove pan from heat, whisk in eggs, parsley and black pepper to taste. Return pan to heat and cook, stirring, for 1 minute. Remove pan from heat, add hot pasta to sauce and toss to combine.
Serve immediately.

Serves 6

ingredients

500g/1 lb fettuccine
<u>Carbonara sauce</u>
250g/8oz ham, prosciutto or bacon, chopped
1/2 cup/125mL/4fl oz chicken stock
1 cup/250mL/8fl oz cream (double)
7 eggs, lightly beaten
2 tablespoons chopped flat-leaf parsley
freshly ground black pepper

hot shallot
& semi-dried tomato pasta

Hot shallot & semi-dried tomato pasta

Serves 4

ingredients

½ **bunch spring onions**
250g/1 lb **bow pasta**
1 **teaspoon butter**
1 **tablespoon olive oil**
1 **small chilli, seeded and sliced**
2 **tablespoons brandy**
300mL/10 fl oz **cream**
⅓ **cup sun-dried tomatoes**
freshly ground black pepper to taste

Method:

1 *Wash and trim spring onions. Slice into 2cm/¾in lengths. Place pasta in boiling water and cook until al dente. Drain, and place in warm serving bowl.*

2 *Heat butter and oil in frying-pan, sauté shallots and chilli for 1 minute. Add brandy, cream and sliced sun-dried tomatoes. Simmer until sauce thickens. Season with pepper.*

3 *Pour over pasta. Serve with Parmesan cheese and sprinkle with freshly ground black pepper.*

traditional lasagne

Method:

1. To make cheese sauce, melt butter in a saucepan over a medium heat. Stir in flour and cook, stirring, for 1 minute. Remove pan from heat and whisk in milk. Return pan to heat and cook, stirring, for 4-5 minutes or until sauce boils and thickens. Stir in cheese and black pepper to taste and set aside.
2. To make meat sauce, heat oil in a frying pan over a medium heat. Add onions and garlic and cook, stirring, for 3 minutes or until onions are soft. Add beef and cook, stirring, for 5 minutes or until beef is brown. Stir in tomatoes, wine and herbs, bring to simmering point and simmer, stirring occasionally, for 15 minutes or until sauce reduces and thickens. Season to taste with black pepper.
3. Line the base of a large greased baking dish with 6 lasagne sheets. Top with one-quarter of the meat sauce and one-quarter of the cheese sauce. Repeat layers to use all ingredients, ending with a layer of cheese sauce.
4. Sprinkle top of lasagne with mozzarella cheese and bake for 30-40 minutes or until it is hot and bubbling and top is golden.

Serves 6

ingredients

24 sheets instant* lasagne
60g/2oz mozzarella cheese, grated

Cheese sauce
75g/2¹/₂oz butter
¹/₃ cup/45g/1¹/₂oz flour
2 cups/500mL/16 fl oz milk
90g/3oz tasty cheese
(mature Cheddar), grated
freshly ground black pepper

Meat sauce
2 teaspoons vegetable oil
2 onions, chopped
2 cloves garlic, crushed
1.25kg/2¹/₂ lb beef mince
2 x 440g/14oz canned tomatoes,
undrained and mashed
³/₄ cup/185mL/6 fl oz red wine
2 tablespoons chopped mixed herbs

*No precooking required

Oven temperature 180°C, 350°F, Gas 4

smoked chicken
pappardelle

Method:

1 To make nasturtium butter, place butter, garlic, lime juice and flowers in a bowl, mix well to combine and set aside.

2 Cook pasta in boiling water in a large saucepan following packet directions. Drain, set aside and keep warm.

3 Heat a non-stick frying pan over a medium heat, add chicken and cook, stirring, for 1 minute. Add wine, cream, chives and black pepper to taste, bring to a simmer and cook for 2 minutes. To serve, top pasta with chicken mixture and nasturtium butter.

Serves 6

ingredients

750g/1 1/2 lb pappardelle
1.5kg/3 lb smoked chicken, skin removed and flesh sliced
1/2 cup/125mL/4 fl oz white wine
1 cup/250mL/8 fl oz cream
2 tablespoons snipped fresh chives
freshly ground black pepper
<u>Nasturtium butter</u>
125g/4oz butter, softened
1 clove garlic, crushed
1 tablespoon lime juice
6 nasturtium flowers, finely chopped

pasta shapes
with avocado sauce

Method:

1. Cook pasta in boiling water in a large saucepan, following packet directions. Drain, set aside and keep warm.
2. To make sauce, place avocado, ricotta cheese, lime juice, lime rind, milk, coriander (cilantro) and black pepper (to taste) in a food processor or blender and process until smooth. Set aside.
3. Boil, steam or microwave snow peas (mangetout) and squash or zucchini (courgettes) separately until just tender. Drain well. Add vegetables to hot pasta and toss to combine. To serve, top pasta with sauce and shavings of Parmesan cheese, if using.

Serves 6

ingredients

500g/1 lb pasta shapes of your choice
125g/4oz snow peas (mangetout), trimmed
125g/4oz yellow squash or zucchini (courgettes), sliced
fresh Parmesan cheese (optional)

Avocado sauce
1 avocado, stoned and peeled
1 cup/250g/8oz ricotta cheese, drained
1 tablespoon lime juice
2 teaspoons finely grated lime rind
2 tablespoons milk
2 tablespoons chopped fresh coriander (cilantro)
freshly ground black pepper

chicken & mango
pasta salad

Method:

1. Cook pasta in boiling water in a large saucepan, following packet directions. Drain, rinse under cold running water, then drain again.
2. Place pasta, chicken, water chestnuts and mangoes in a bowl and toss to combine.
3. To make dressing, place mayonnaise, chutney, spring onions, coriander (cilantro) and black pepper (to taste) in a bowl and mix to combine. Spoon dressing over salad and toss to combine. Cover and chill until required.

Serves 6

ingredients

500g/1 lb large shell pasta
Flesh of 1 cooked chicken, cut into bite-sized pieces
220g/7oz canned water chestnuts, drained and sliced
440g/14oz canned mangoes, drained and sliced

Mango chutney dressing
1 cup/250g/8oz low-fat mayonnaise
½ cup/155g/5oz sweet mango chutney
2 spring onions, finely chopped
2 tablespoons chopped fresh coriander (cilantro)
freshly ground black pepper

gnocchi
with gorgonzola sauce

ingredients

500g/1 lb potato gnocchi
<u>Gorgonzola sauce</u>
200g/6¹/₂oz Gorgonzola or blue cheese, crumbled
¾ cup/185mL/6fl oz milk
60g/2oz butter
60g/2oz walnuts, toasted and chopped
200mL/6¹/₂fl oz thickened cream (double)
freshly ground black pepper

Method:

1. Cook gnocchi in boiling water in a large saucepan, following packet directions. Drain, set aside and keep warm.
2. To make sauce, place Gorgonzola or blue cheese, milk and butter in a saucepan and cook over low heat, stirring, for 4-5 minutes or until cheese melts. Stir in walnuts, cream and black pepper to taste. Bring to a simmer and cook for 5 minutes or until sauce reduces and thickens. Spoon sauce over hot gnocchi and toss to combine.

Serves 6

---

spaghetti
bolognaise

ingredients

500g/1 lb spaghetti
grated Parmesan cheese (optional)
<u>Bolognaise sauce</u>
2 teaspoons vegetable oil
1 clove garlic, crushed
1 onion, chopped
500g/1 lb beef mince
440g/14oz canned tomato purée (passata)
¼ cup/60mL/2fl oz red wine or water
1 tablespoon chopped fresh oregano or ¹/₂ teaspoon dried oregano
1 tablespoon chopped fresh thyme or ¹/₂ teaspoon dried thyme
freshly ground black pepper

Method:

1. To make sauce, heat oil in a frying pan over a medium heat. Add garlic and onion and cook, stirring, for 3 minutes or until onion is soft.
2. Add beef and cook, stirring, for 5 minutes or until meat is well browned. Stir in tomato purée (passata), wine or water, oregano and thyme. Bring to a simmer and cook, stirring occasionally, for 15 minutes or until sauce reduces and thickens. Season to taste with black pepper.
3. Cook pasta in boiling water in a large saucepan following packet directions. Drain well. To serve, spoon sauce over hot pasta and top with Parmesan cheese.

Serves 4

chicken
pasta toss

Method:

1 Cook pasta in boiling water in a large saucepan, following packet directions. Drain, set aside and keep warm.

2 Melt butter in a large frying pan and cook onion and garlic, stirring, over a medium heat for 3-4 minutes. Add chicken and stock, and cook for 4-5 minutes longer.

3 Add spinach and pasta to pan, season to taste with black pepper and toss to combine. Sprinkle with pine nuts and serve immediately.

Serves 4

ingredients

500g/1 lb shell pasta
30g/1oz butter
1 onion, finely chopped
1 clove garlic, crushed
250g/8oz cooked chicken, shredded
½ cup/125mL/4fl oz chicken stock
6 spinach leaves, shredded
freshly ground black pepper
60g/2oz pine nuts, toasted

pepperoni
toss

Method:

1 Cook spaghetti in boiling water in a large saucepan, following packet directions. Drain, set aside and keep warm.

2 Heat oil in a large frying pan and cook onion over a medium heat for 5-6 minutes or until onion is transparent. Add olives and salami and cook for 2 minutes longer.

3 Add spaghetti to pan and toss to combine. Serve immediately.

Serves 6

ingredients

375g/12oz spaghetti
1 tablespoon olive oil
1 onion, finely chopped
90g/3oz black olives, chopped
125g/4oz pepperoni salami, chopped

spirelli with ham

Method:

1. Cook spirelli in boiling water in a large saucepan, following packet directions. Drain, set aside and keep warm.
2. Heat oil in a frying pan and cook ham and artichokes for 1-2 minutes.
3. Add spirelli to pan and toss to combine. Remove from heat and quickly stir in egg mixture. Season to taste with black pepper. Serve as soon as the eggs start to stick to spirelli – this will take only a few seconds.

Serves 4

ingredients

500g/1 lb fresh or 410g/13oz dried spirelli or spiral pasta
2 teaspoons olive oil
315g/10oz ham, cut into strips
6 canned artichoke hearts, sliced lengthwise
3 eggs, beaten with 1 tablespoon grated fresh Parmesan cheese
freshly ground black pepper

spaghetti
carbonara

Method:

1. Cook ham in a non-stick frying pan for 2-3 minutes. Place eggs, cream and Parmesan cheese in a bowl and beat lightly to combine.
2. Cook spaghetti in boiling water in a large saucepan following packet directions. Drain spaghetti, add egg mixture and ham and toss so that the heat of the spaghetti cooks the sauce. Season to taste with black pepper and serve immediately.

Serves 4

ingredients

185g/6oz slices ham, cut into strips
4 eggs
1/3 cup/90mL/3fl oz pure cream (single)
90g/3oz grated fresh Parmesan cheese
500g/1 lb spaghetti
freshly ground black pepper

warm pasta
and salami salad

Method:

1. Cook pasta in boiling water in a large saucepan, following packet directions. Drain, set aside and keep warm.

2. Heat oil in a large frying pan and cook garlic and pine nuts, stirring constantly, over a medium heat for 1-2 minutes. Remove pan from heat and stir in salami and parsley. Add salami mixture to pasta and toss to combine. Serve while still warm.

Serves 4 as a light meal

ingredients

250g/8oz large shell pasta
1 tablespoon olive oil
2 cloves garlic, crushed
60g/2oz pine nuts
125g/4oz salami, thinly sliced
1 tablespoon chopped fresh parsley

pork-and-sage
filled ravioli

Method:

1 To make filling, place ricotta cheese, bacon, pork, parsley, sage and Parmesan cheese in a bowl. Mix to combine and season to taste with nutmeg and black pepper. Cover and set aside while making pasta.

Assemble, following directions for making ravioli.

ingredients

1 quantity Homemade Pasta dough (see recipe page 75)
grated fresh Parmesan cheese

Pork and sage filling
315g/10oz ricotta cheese, drained
60g/2oz lean bacon, finely chopped
155g/5oz lean cooked pork, finely diced
1 teaspoon finely chopped fresh parsley
1/2 teaspoon finely chopped fresh sage
1 teaspoon grated fresh Parmesan cheese
grated nutmeg
freshly ground black pepper

chicken pasta salad

Method:

1. Cook plain, spinach and tomato tagliatelle together in boiling water in a large saucepan, following packet directions. Drain, rinse under cold running water, then drain again and set aside to cool completely.
2. Heat oil in a large frying pan and cook onions and garlic, stirring, over a medium heat for 2-3 minutes. Add chicken, oregano and basil and cook, stirring, for 10 minutes longer or until chicken is cooked. Remove pan from heat and set aside to cool completely. Place cooked chicken mixture, artichokes, red capsicum (pepper), olives and tagliatelle in a large salad bowl. Season to taste with black pepper and toss to combine.

Serves 6

ingredients

155g/5oz plain tagliatelle
155g/5oz spinach tagliatelle
155g/5oz tomato tagliatelle
2 tablespoons olive oil
2 red onions, cut into eighths
2 cloves garlic, crushed
500g/1 lb chicken breast fillets, chopped
1 tablespoon finely chopped fresh oregano or 1 teaspoon dried oregano
1 tablespoon finely chopped fresh basil or 1 teaspoon dried basil
440g/14oz canned artichoke hearts, drained and halved
1 red capsicum (pepper), cut into strips
90g/3oz green olives, drained
freshly ground black pepper

vegetable pasta salad

Photograph Page 39

Method:

1. Cook pasta in boiling water in a large saucepan, following packet directions. Drain, rinse under cold running water, then drain again and set aside to cool completely.
2. Boil, steam or microwave broccoli for 2-3 minutes or until it just changes colour. Refresh under cold running water. Drain, then dry on absorbent kitchen paper.
3. To make dressing, place vinegar, oil, Parmesan cheese, garlic and black pepper to taste in a screw-top jar and shake to combine.
4. Place pasta, broccoli, tomatoes, spring onions and olives in a salad bowl. Pour dressing over and toss to combine.

Serves 8

ingredients

500g/1 lb small pasta shapes of your choice
250g/8oz broccoli, broken into florets
250g/8oz cherry tomatoes, halved
6 spring onions, cut into 2.5cm/1in lengths
12 black olives

Red wine dressing
2 tablespoons red wine vinegar
1/4 cup/125mL/4fl oz olive oil
2 tablespoons grated fresh Parmesan cheese
1 clove garlic, crushed
freshly ground black pepper

meat & poultry

seafood

Spaghetti with tuna and cress

Seafood and pasta team well together,

as do their nutritional values. The high-protein low-fat seafood combined with the complex-carbohydrate pasta make a nutritionally well-balanced meal. Add a tossed salad to complete your nutritional requirements. Shellfish is a wonderful ingredient for pasta dishes. Quick to cook, attractive to serve, and a delight to eat, what could be better than seafood pasta and a glass of good wine? Fresh fish or canned varieties are equally suitable to use. Simmer your favourite seafood in any of the wide range of sauces provided in this book and serve with your favourite pasta.

scallop
and capsicum pasta

Method:

1. To make Gremolata, place garlic, parsley and lemon rind in a bowl and mix well to combine.
2. Cook pasta in boiling water in a large saucepan, following packet directions. Drain, set aside and keep warm.
3. Heat oil in a frying pan over a medium heat. Add scallops and prosciutto or ham and cook, stirring, for 3 minutes or until scallops just turn opaque and prosciutto or ham is crisp. Remove pan from heat, stir in lemon juice, basil and black pepper to taste and set aside.
4. Place stock in a saucepan, bring to a simmer and cook until reduced by half. Add red capsicum (pepper) and leeks and simmer for 3 minutes. Add pasta and scallop mixture to stock mixture. Toss to combine and top with Gremolata.

Serves 4

ingredients

500g/1 lb tagliarini
1 tablespoon olive oil
500g/1 lb scallops
100g/3½oz prosciutto or lean ham, cut into thin strips
2 tablespoons lemon juice
2 tablespoons chopped fresh basil or 1 teaspoon dried basil
freshly ground black pepper
1 cup/250mL/8fl oz chicken stock
1 red capsicum(pepper), cut into strips
2 leeks, cut into strips
Gremolata
3 cloves garlic, crushed
½ bunch flat-leaf parsley, leaves finely chopped
1 tablespoon finely grated lemon rind

spaghetti
with tuna & cress

Photograph Page 41

Method:

1. Cook pasta in boiling water in a large saucepan of boiling water, following packet directions. Drain well and place in a large serving bowl.
2. Add tuna, watercress, olives, lime rind, ginger, vinegar, oil and lime juice to hot pasta and toss to combine. Serve immediately.

Serves 4

ingredients

500g/1 lb spaghetti
500g/1 lb tuna steaks, thinly sliced
1 bunch/250g/8oz watercress, leaves removed and stems discarded
125g/4oz black olives
1 tablespoon finely grated lime rind
2 teaspoons finely grated fresh ginger
¼ cup/60mL/2fl oz balsamic or red wine vinegar
1 tablespoon olive oil
2 tablespoons lime juice

raspberry
salmon pasta

Method:

1. To make mayonnaise, place raspberries in a food processor or blender and process until smooth. Push purée through a fine sieve and discard seeds. Add mayonnaise, mustard and lemon juice to purée, mix to combine and set aside.
2. Cook pasta in boiling water in a large saucepan, following packet directions. Drain, set aside and keep warm.
3. Heat oil in a frying or grill pan over a medium heat. Brush salmon with lemon juice and sprinkle with dill. Place salmon in pan and cook for 2-3 minutes each side or until flesh flakes when tested with a fork. Remove salmon from pan and cut into thick slices.
4. To serve, divide pasta between six serving plates. Top with salmon slices and drizzle with raspberry mayonnaise. Serve immediately.

Serves 6

ingredients

500g/1 lb pepper or plain fettuccine
1 tablespoon vegetable oil
500g/1 lb salmon fillet, bones and skin removed
2 tablespoons lemon juice
2 tablespoons chopped fresh dill

Raspberry mayonnaise
200g/6½oz raspberries
1 cup/250g/8oz low-fat mayonnaise
2 teaspoons wholegrain mustard
1 tablespoon lemon juice

lobster
in pasta nets

ingredients

375g/12oz angel-hair pasta
3 uncooked lobster tails, shelled and flesh cut into 4 cm/1 1/2in pieces,
flour
vegetable oil for deep frying
Lime cream
1/2 cup/125g/4oz mayonnaise
1/4 cup/60g/2oz sour cream
1 tablespoon finely grated lime rind
1 tablespoon lime juice
1 tablespoon wholegrain mustard
2 tablespoons chopped fresh tarragon or 1 teaspoon dried tarragon

Method:

1 Cook pasta in boiling water in a large saucepan until almost cooked. Drain, rinse under cold running water, drain again and pat dry on absorbent kitchen paper. Set aside.
2 To make lime cream, place mayonnaise, sour cream, lime rind, lime juice, mustard and tarragon in a bowl and mix to combine. Set aside.
3 Dust lobster pieces with flour. Wrap a few stands of pasta around each lobster piece. Continue wrapping with pasta to form a net effect around lobster.
4 Heat oil in a large saucepan until a cube of bread dropped in browns in 50 seconds. Cook pasta-wrapped lobster in batches for 2-3 minutes or until golden. Drain on absorbent kitchen paper and serve immediately with lime cream.

Lobster in pasta nets

Serves 4

avocado
salmon salad

ingredients

375g/12oz bow pasta
1 large avocado, stoned, peeled and roughly chopped
1 teaspoon finely grated orange rind
2 tablespoons fresh orange juice
freshly ground black pepper
4 slices smoked salmon
4 sprigs fresh dill
1 orange, segmented

Method:

1 Cook pasta in boiling water in a large saucepan, following packet directions. Drain, rinse under cold running water, then drain again and set aside to cool completely.
2 Place avocado, orange rind, orange juice and black pepper (to taste) in a food processor or blender and process until smooth.
3 Place pasta in a bowl, top with avocado mixture and toss to combine. Roll salmon slices into cornets and fill with a dill sprig. Divide salad between four serving plates and top with salmon cornets and orange segments.

Serves 4 as a light meal

pasta with broccoli
and anchovy sauce

Method:
1. Cook broccoli florets in boiling water for 1-2 minutes, ensuring they are still crisp.
2. In a frying-pan heat the oil. Cook anchovy fillets and garlic slivers, stirring until anchovies disintegrate. Stir in the chilli and add cooked broccoli and pepper to taste.
3. Meanwhile, cook the pasta in boiling, salted water until al dente. Drain and add sauce. Mix carefully and serve

Serves 4-6

ingredients

500g/1lb broccoli, cut into florets
125mL/4fl oz olive oil
6 anchovy fillets, drained
3 garlic cloves, peeled and thinly sliced
1/2 teaspoon freshly chopped chilli
freshly ground black pepper
410g/13oz pasta of choice

quick fettuccine
with scallops

Method:

1. Cook fettuccine in boiling water in a large saucepan, following packet directions. Drain, set aside and keep warm.
2. To make sauce, melt butter in a large frying pan and cook red capsicum (pepper) and spring onions for 1-2 minutes. Add cream and bring to the boil, then reduce heat and simmer for 5 minutes or until sauce reduces slightly and thickens.
3. Stir scallops into sauce and cook for 2-3 minutes or until scallops are opaque. Season to taste with black pepper. Place fettuccine in a warm serving bowl, top with sauce and sprinkle with parsley.

Serves 4

ingredients

500g/1 lb fettuccine
<u>Scallop sauce</u>
30g/1oz butter
1 red capsicum (pepper), cut into strips
2 spring onions, finely chopped
1 cup/250mL/8 fl oz thickened cream (double)
500g/1 lb scallops
freshly ground black pepper
1 tablespoon finely chopped fresh parsley

tagliatelle
with chilli octopus

Method:
1. To make marinade, place sesame oil, ginger, lime juice and chilli sauce in a large bowl and mix to combine. Add octopus, tossing to coat, then cover and marinate in the refrigerator for 3-4 hours.
2. Cook pasta in boiling water in a large saucepan, following packet directions. Drain, set aside and keep warm.
3. To make sauce, heat oil in a saucepan over a medium heat. Add spring onions and cook, stirring, for 1 minute. Stir in tomato purée (passata), bring to a simmer and cook for 4 minutes.
4. Cook octopus under a preheated hot grill for 5-7 minutes or until tender. Add octopus to sauce and toss to combine. Spoon octopus mixture over hot pasta and toss to combine.

Serves 4

ingredients

1kg/2 lb baby octopus, cleaned
500g/1 lb spinach tagliatelle
Chilli ginger marinade
1 tablespoon sesame oil
1 tablespoon grated fresh ginger
2 tablespoons lime juice
2 tablespoon sweet chilli sauce
Tomato sauce
2 teaspoons vegetable oil
3 spring onions, sliced diagonally
440g/14oz canned tomato purée (passata)

pasta shells
with anchovy sauce

Method:
1. Cook pasta shells in boiling water in a large saucepan, following packet directions. Drain, set aside and keep warm.
2. To make sauce, heat oil in a large frying pan and cook onions and garlic over a medium heat for 10 minutes or until onions are soft. Stir in wine and anchovies and bring to the boil. Cook for 2-3 minutes or until wine reduces by half.
3. Stir in rosemary and stock and bring back to the boil. Cook until sauces reduces and thickens slightly. Add chilli and pasta to sauce, toss to combine, sprinkle with Parmesan cheese and serve immediately.

Serves 4

ingredients

500g/1 lb small shell pasta
60g/2oz grated fresh Parmesan cheese
Anchovy sauce
2 tablespoons olive oil
3 onions, chopped
1 clove garlic, crushed
1/2 cup/125mL/4fl oz dry white wine
8 canned anchovies
1 tablespoon chopped fresh rosemary leaves or 1 teaspoon dried rosemary
1 cup/250mL/8fl oz beef or chicken stock
1 fresh red chilli, seeded and cut into rings

---

macaroni
with tomato sauce
Photograph Page 49

Method:
1. Cook macaroni in boiling water in a large saucepan, following packet directions. Drain, set aside and keep warm.
2. To make sauce, heat oil in a frying pan and cook onion for 3-4 minutes or until soft. Stir in garlic, tomatoes and wine and cook, stirring constantly, over a medium heat for 5 minutes. Bring to the boil, then reduce heat and simmer, uncovered, for 10-15 minutes or until sauce reduces and thickens. Add basil and season to taste with black pepper.
3. Add sauce to hot macaroni and toss to combine. Serve immediately.

Serves 4

ingredients

500g/1 lb wholemeal macaroni
Chunky tomato sauce
2 tablespoons olive oil
1 onion, chopped
1 clove garlic, crushed
2 x 440g/14oz canned Italian-style tomatoes, undrained and mashed
1/4 cup/60mL/2fl oz dry white wine
1 tablespoon chopped fresh basil
freshly ground black pepper

oriental
vegetable noodles

Method:

1. Cook noodles in boiling water in a large saucepan following packet directions. Drain and set aside to keep warm.
2. Heat oil in a wok or large frying pan over a high heat, add garlic, ginger, fish and prawns and stir-fry for 2 minutes or until prawns just change colour.
3. Add spring onions, red capsicum (pepper) and bok choy (Chinese cabbage) to pan and stir-fry for 3 minutes longer. Add sweet corn, snow peas (mangetout), and mushrooms and stir-fry for 3 minutes.
4. Add mint, chilli sauce, soy sauce, plum sauce, lime juice and noodles and stir-fry for 3 minutes or until heated through. Serve immediately.

ingredients

315 g/10 oz fresh egg noodles
1 tablespoon sesame oil
1 clove garlic, crushed
1 tablespoon grated fresh ginger
185 g/6 oz firm white fish fillets, cut into 2 cm/3/4 in pieces
155 g/5 oz green prawns, shelled and deveined
4 spring onions, sliced
1 red capsicum (pepper), sliced
250 g/8 oz bok choy (Chinese cabbage), chopped
375 g/12 oz canned whole baby sweet corn,
125 g/4 oz snow peas (mangetout)
125 g/4 oz fresh shiitake mushrooms, sliced
2 tablespoons chopped fresh mint
2 tablespoons sweet chilli sauce
2 tablespoons sweet soy sauce
1 tablespoon plum sauce
1 tablespoon lime juice

pasta
with anchovies & basil sauce

Method:

1. Heat the oil and sauté garlic and anchovies until garlic is only just yellow in colour. Turn heat to very low, and then toss halved tomatoes, basil leaves, sun-dried tomatoes and capers in with the anchovies and oil.
2. Cook pasta in boiling, salted water until al dente and drain thoroughly. Pour sauce over fresh pasta and garnish with fresh chopped basil and sprinkle black pepper to taste.

Serves 4

ingredients

250mL/8fl oz olive oil
2 cloves garlic, crushed
8 anchovy fillets, reserve oil
2 punnets cherry tomatoes, halved
20 fresh basil leaves, roughly chopped
12 sun-dried tomatoes, sliced
2 teaspoons capers
500g/1 lb egg fettuccine
½ cup fresh basil, chopped
freshly ground black pepper

penne with tuna
olives & artichokes

Method:

1. *Cook the pasta in boiling salted water until al dente. Drain, and rinse in cold water.*
2. *Heat 2 tablespoons of the oil in a pan, add the garlic and chilli, and cook for 2-3 minutes. Return the cooked pasta to the pan, add the remaining ingredients and heat through.*
3. *Serve immediately with Parmesan cheese.*

Serves 4-6

ingredients

500g/1 lb penne pasta
6 tablespoons olive oil
2 cloves garlic, minced
3 chillies, seeded and finely chopped
1 cup black olives, seeded
400g/13oz can artichokes
2 tablespoons capers, finely chopped
425g/14oz can tuna, drained

tuna-filled shells

Method:

1. Cook 8 pasta shells in a large saucepan of boiling water until al dente. Drain, rinse under cold running water and drain again. Set aside, then repeat with remaining shells, ensure cooked shells do not overlap.
2. To make filling, place ricotta cheese and tuna in a bowl and mix to combine. Mix in red capsicum (pepper), capers, chives and 2 tablespoons grated Swiss cheese, nutmeg and black pepper to taste.
3. Fill each shell with ricotta mixture, and place in a lightly greased, shallow ovenproof dish. Sprinkle with Parmesan cheese and remaining Swiss cheese. Place under a preheated grill and cook until cheese melts.

Makes 16

ingredients

16 giant pasta shells
<u>Tuna filling</u>
250g/8oz ricotta cheese, drained
440g/14oz canned tuna in brine, drained and flaked
½ red capsicum (pepper), diced
1 tablespoon chopped capers
1 teaspoon snipped fresh chives
4 tablespoons grated Swiss cheese
pinch ground nutmeg
freshly ground black pepper
2 tablespoons grated fresh Parmesan cheese

vegetables

llnguine with chilli and lemon

A healthy way to enjoy pasta is with

vegetable sauces. Any vegetable combination enriched with fresh herbs, spiced up with garlic, chilli or curry, may be tossed through your favourite pasta.

Vegetarian eating has become increasingly popular. Whether it's the committed vegetarian or simply the cook looking for new and interesting ways to make the most of fresh vegetables and delicious pasta, there are recipes that will appeal in this chapter.

You will also discover that Italy is not the only country with a cuisine that includes pasta – many European countries also have wonderful pasta dishes. Of course, there is also Oriental pasta which includes such delicacies as Chinese egg and rice noodles and Japanese soba noodles.

No matter the flavour or type of noodle here are recipes to suit every taste and occasion.

fettuccine
with spinach sauce

Method:
1. Cook pasta in boiling water in a large saucepan, following packet directions. Drain, set aside and keep warm.
2. To make sauce, melt butter in a saucepan over a medium heat, add garlic and leek and cook, stirring, for 3 minutes. Add spinach and cook for 3 minutes longer or until spinach wilts.
3. Place spinach mixture, cream cheese, grated Parmesan cheese and stock in a food processor or blender and process until smooth. Return sauce to a clean saucepan, bring to a simmer and cook, stirring constantly, for 5-6 minutes or until sauce thickens and is heated through.
4. Spoon sauce over hot pasta and toss to combine. Serve topped with shavings of Parmesan cheese.

Serves 4

ingredients

500g/1 lb fettuccine
fresh Parmesan cheese
<u>Spinach sauce</u>
15g/½oz butter
1 clove garlic, crushed
1 leek, sliced
500g/1 lb English spinach, chopped
250g/8oz low-fat cream cheese
2 tablespoons grated Parmesan cheese
½ cup/125mL/4fl oz chicken stock

linguine
with chilli & lemon

Photograph Page 55

Method:
1. Cook pasta in boiling water in a large saucepan, following packet directions. Drain, set aside and keep warm.
2. Heat oil in a frying pan over a low heat, add garlic and chillies and cook, stirring, for 6 minutes or until garlic is golden. Add garlic mixture, rocket (arugola), lemon rind, lemon juice, black pepper (to taste) and Parmesan cheese to hot pasta and toss to combine.

Serves 4

ingredients

500g/1 lb fresh linguine or spaghetti
2 tablespoons olive oil
6 cloves garlic, peeled
2 fresh red chillies, seeded and sliced
125g/4oz rocket (arugola), shredded
3 teaspoons finely grated lemon rind
2 tablespoons lemon juice
freshly ground black pepper
90g/3oz grated Parmesan cheese

penne napolitana

Method:

1. Cook pasta in boiling water in a large saucepan, following packet directions. Drain, set aside and keep warm.
2. To make sauce, heat oil in a saucepan over a medium heat. Add onions and garlic and cook, stirring, for 3 minutes or until onions are soft.
3. Stir in tomatoes, wine, parsley, oregano and black pepper to taste. Bring to a simmer and cook for 15 minutes or until sauce reduces and thickens.
4. To serve, spoon sauce over hot pasta and top with shavings of Parmesan cheese.

Serves 4

ingredients

500g/1 lb penne
fresh Parmesan cheese
<u>**Napolitana sauce**</u>
2 teaspoons olive oil
2 onions, chopped
2 cloves garlic, crushed
2 x 440g/14oz canned tomatoes, undrained and mashed
3/4 cup/185mL/6fl oz red wine
1 tablespoon chopped flat-leaf parsley
1 tablespoon chopped fresh oregano or 1/2 teaspoon dried oregano
freshly ground black pepper

fettuccine pesto

Method:

1. Cook pasta in boiling water in a large saucepan, following packet directions. Drain, set aside and keep warm.
2. To make pesto, place Parmesan cheese, garlic, pine nuts and basil in a food processor or blender and process to finely chop. With machine running, gradually add oil and continue processing to form a smooth paste. To serve, spoon pesto over hot pasta and toss to combine.

Serves 4

ingredients

500g/1 lb fettuccine

<u>Basil pesto</u>
100g/3½oz fresh Parmesan cheese, chopped
2 cloves garlic, crushed
60g/2oz pine nuts
1 large bunch basil, leaves removed and stems discarded
¼ cup/60mL/2fl oz olive oil

vegetable
& chilli pasta

Method:

1. Cut eggplant (aubergines) into 2cm/³⁄₄in cubes. Place in a colander, sprinkle with salt and set aside to drain for 10 minutes. Rinse eggplant under cold running water and pat dry.
2. Cook pasta in boiling water in a large saucepan, following packet directions. Drain, set aside and keep warm.
3. Heat oil in a large frying pan over a medium heat and cook eggplant in batches, for 5 minutes or until golden. Remove eggplant from pan, drain on absorbent kitchen paper and set aside.
4. Add onions, chillies and garlic to pan and cook, stirring, for 3 minutes or until onions are golden. Stir in tomatoes, wine and basil, bring to a simmer and cook for 5 minutes. To serve, spoon sauce over hot pasta.

Serves 4

ingredients

2 eggplant, (aubergines)
salt
500g/1 lb pasta shells
¼ cup/60mL/2fl oz olive oil
2 onions, chopped
2 fresh red chillies, seeded and chopped
2 cloves garlic, crushed
2 x 440g/14oz canned tomatoes, undrained and mashed
½ cup/125mL/4fl oz dry white wine
2 tablespoons chopped fresh basil or
1 teaspoon dried basil

tortellini
& avocado cream

Method:

1. Cook tortellini in boiling water in a large saucepan following packet directions. Drain, set aside and keep warm.
2. To make Avocado Cream, place avocado, cream, Parmesan cheese and lemon juice in a food processor or blender and process until smooth. Season to taste with black pepper.
3. Place tortellini in a warm serving bowl, add Avocado Cream and toss to combine. Serve immediately.

Serves 4

ingredients

500g/1 lb tortellini
AVOCADO CREAM
¹/₂ ripe avocado, stoned and peeled
¹/₄ cup/60mL/2fl oz cream (double)
30g/1oz grated fresh Parmesan cheese
1 teaspoon lemon juice
freshly ground black pepper

rigatoni
with pumpkin

Method:

1. Cook rigatoni in boiling water in a large saucepan, following packet directions. Drain, set aside and keep warm.
2. Melt 60g/2oz butter in a large saucepan and cook pumpkin over a medium heat for 5-10 minutes or until tender.
3. Stir chives, nutmeg, Parmesan cheese, black pepper (to taste), rigatoni and remaining butter into pumpkin mixture and toss to combine. Serve immediately.

Serves 4

ingredients

500g/1 lb rigatoni
90g/3oz butter
250g/8oz pumpkin, cut into small cubes
1 tablespoon snipped fresh chives
pinch ground nutmeg
30g/1oz grated fresh Parmesan cheese
freshly ground black pepper

vegetables

macaroni
with basil

Method:
1. Cook macaroni in boiling water in a large saucepan, following packet directions. Drain, set aside and keep warm.
2. Heat oil in a large frying pan and cook garlic, mushrooms and tomatoes over a medium heat for 4-5 minutes. Stir in basil and season to taste with black pepper.
3. Add macaroni to mushroom mixture and toss to combine. Serve immediately.

Serves 4

ingredients

375g/12oz wholemeal macaroni
1 tablespoon olive oil
2 cloves garlic, crushed
250g/8oz button mushrooms, sliced
6 sun-dried tomatoes, drained and cut into strips
2 tablespoons chopped fresh basil
freshly ground black pepper

chilli broad bean salad

Method:

1. Cook pasta in boiling water in a large saucepan, following packet directions. Drain, rinse under cold running water, then drain again and set aside to cool completely.
2. Heat oil in a large frying pan and cook broad beans and chilli paste over a medium heat for 3 minutes. Stir in stock, bring to a simmer, cover and cook for 10 minutes. Drain off any remaining liquid and set aside to cool.
3. To make dressing, place oil, vinegar, garlic and black pepper to taste in a screw-top jar. Shake well to combine.
4. Place pasta, broad bean mixture, radishes, parsley and Parmesan cheese in a salad bowl. Pour dressing over and toss to combine.

Serves 4

ingredients

375g/12oz small shell pasta
1 tablespoon vegetable oil
250g/8oz shelled or frozen broad beans
1 teaspoon chilli paste (sambal selek)
1 1/2 cups/375mL/12fl oz chicken stock
6 radishes, thinly sliced
2 tablespoons chopped fresh parsley
30g/1oz grated fresh Parmesan cheese

Garlic dressing
1/4 cup/60mL/2fl oz olive oil
1 tablespoon cider vinegar
1 clove garlic, crushed
freshly ground black pepper

ravioli
with lemon sauce

Method:

1. Cook pasta in boiling water in a large saucepan, following packet directions. Drain, set aside and keep warm.
2. To make sauce, melt butter in a frying pan over a low heat, add garlic and cook, stirring, for 1 minute. Stir in cream, lemon juice, Parmesan cheese, chives and lemon rind, bring to a simmer and cook for 2 minutes. Add parsley and black pepper to taste and cook for 1 minute longer. Spoon sauce over pasta and toss to combine. Scatter with almonds and serve.

Serves 4

ingredients

500g/1 lb cheese and spinach ravioli
30g/1oz slivered almonds, toasted

<u>Lemon cream sauce</u>
30g/1oz butter
1 clove garlic, crushed
1¼ cups/315mL/10fl oz thickened (double) cream
¼ cup/60mL/2fl oz lemon juice
30g/1oz grated fresh Parmesan cheese
3 tablespoons snipped fresh chives
1 teaspoon finely grated lemon rind
2 tablespoons chopped fresh parsley
freshly ground black pepper

fettuccine
with corn sauce

Method:

1. Cook pasta in boiling water in a large saucepan, following packet directions. Drain, set aside and keep warm.

2. To make sauce, heat oil in a saucepan over a medium heat, add red capsicum (pepper) and cook, stirring, for 2 minutes or until capsicum (pepper) is soft. Stir in sweet corn, water, chilli sauce, coriander and black pepper to taste and cook for 2 minutes longer or until sauce is hot. Spoon sauce over pasta and toss to combine.

Serves 4

ingredients

500g/1 lb fresh fettuccine
<u>Corn and coriander sauce</u>
1 tablespoon olive oil
1 red capsicum (pepper), chopped
440g/14oz canned creamed sweet corn
¼ cup/60mL/2fl oz water
2 teaspoons hot chilli sauce
2 tablespoons chopped fresh coriander
freshly ground black pepper

crests
with mushrooms

Method:

1 Cook pasta in boiling water in a large saucepan, following packet directions. Drain, set aside and keep warm.

2 To make sauce, melt butter in a saucepan over a medium heat, add mushrooms, onion and garlic and cook, stirring occasionally, for 5 minutes or until onions and mushrooms are soft.

3 Stir in paprika, wine and tomato paste (purée), bring to a simmer and cook for 5 minutes. Remove pan from heat, stir in sour cream and parsley and cook over a low heat for 3-4 minutes or until heated through. Season to taste with black pepper. Spoon sauce over pasta and serve immediately.

Serves 4

ingredients

375g/12oz cresti di gallo pasta
Mushroom and paprika sauce
30g/1oz butter
125g/4oz mushrooms, sliced
1 onion, thinly sliced
1 clove garlic, crushed
1 tablespoon ground paprika
1/2 cup/125mL/4fl oz white wine
2 tablespoons tomato paste (purée)
1 1/4 cups/315g/10oz sour cream
1 tablespoon chopped fresh parsley or
1 teaspoon dried parsley flakes
freshly ground black pepper

tomato & cheese lasagne

Method:

1. Place ricotta cheese, parsley, basil and black pepper (to taste) in a bowl and mix to combine. Set aside.
2. Place pecorino or Parmesan and mozzarella cheeses in a bowl and mix to combine. Set aside.
3. To make sauce, heat oil in a saucepan over a medium heat, add garlic and onion and cook, stirring, for 3 minutes or until onion is soft. Add tomatoes and cook, stirring for 4 minutes longer.
4. Add tomato paste (purée), bay leaf, thyme, ham or bacon bone, water and sugar and bring to the boil. Reduce heat and simmer, stirring occasionally, for 45 minutes or until sauce reduces and thickens. Remove ham or bacon bone from sauce and discard.
5. Place three lasagne sheets in the base of a greased 18x28cm/7x11in ovenproof dish. Top with one-third of the tomato sauce, then one-third of the ricotta mixture and one-third of the cheese mixture. Repeat layers twice more to use all ingredients, finishing with a layer of cheese. Bake for 30 minutes or until hot and bubbling and top is golden.

Serves 6

ingredients

1 cup/250g/8oz ricotta cheese, drained
1 tablespoon chopped fresh parsley
1 tablespoon chopped fresh basil
freshly ground black pepper
60g/2oz grated pecorino or Parmesan cheese
125g/4oz grated mozzarella cheese
9 sheets instant* lasagne

Fresh tomato sauce
2 teaspoons olive oil
2 cloves garlic, crushed
1 onion, chopped
7 tomatoes, peeled, seeded and chopped
2 tablespoons tomato paste (purée)
1 bay leaf
3 sprigs fresh thyme or
1/2 teaspoon dried thyme
1 small ham or bacon bone
1/2 cup/125mL/4fl oz water
1 teaspoon sugar

*No pre-cooking required

grilled vegetable salad

grilled vegetable salad

Serves 6

ingredients

250g/8oz fresh angel-hair pasta
1 large eggplant (aubergine)
salt
1 large red capsicum (pepper), seeded and quartered
1 large green capsicum (pepper), seeded and quartered
4 spring onions, sliced diagonally

Sesame and chilli dressing
2 fresh red chillies, seeded and diced
1 clove garlic, crushed
¹/₂ cup/125mL/4fl oz olive oil
¹/₃ cup/90mL/3fl oz soy sauce
2 tablespoons sesame oil
2 tablespoons honey
2 tablespoons red wine vinegar

Method:

1. Cook pasta in boiling water in a large saucepan, following packet directions. Drain and rinse under cold running water. Drain again and set aside.

2. Cut eggplant (aubergine) into 1cm/¹/₂in-thick slices and place in a colander. Sprinkle with salt and set aside for 1 hour. Rinse eggplant under cold running water, then pat dry with absorbent kitchen paper.

3. To make dressing, place chillies, garlic, olive oil, soy sauce, sesame oil, honey and vinegar in a bowl and whisk to combine.

4. Brush eggplant slices with some of the dressing and cook under a preheated hot grill for 5 minutes each side or until golden. Set aside to cool, then cut into strips.

5. Place red and green capsicum (pepper) quarters, skin side up, under a hot grill and cook for 5-10 minutes or until skins are blistered and charred. Place capsicums in a plastic or paper bag and set aside until cool enough to handle. Remove skins and cut flesh into chunks.

6. Place pasta, eggplant, red and green capsicums, and spring onions in a large bowl and toss gently. Pour over remaining dressing and toss to coat pasta and vegetables. Cover and chill until required.

tortellini
with onion confit

Method:

1 To make confit, melt butter in a saucepan over a medium heat, add onions and cook, stirring, for 3 minutes or until onions are soft. Stir in sugar and cook for 2 minutes longer. Add thyme, wine and vinegar, bring to a simmer and cookr, stirring frequently, for 40 minutes or until mixture reduces and thickens.

2 Place stock in a saucepan, bring to the boil and cook until reduced by half. Keep warm.

3 Cook pasta in boiling water in a large saucepan, following packet directions. Drain well. Add pasta, confit, peas and tarragon to stock, bring to a simmer and cook for 2-3 minutes or until peas are just cooked.

Serves 4

ingredients

1¹/₂ cups/375mL/12fl oz beef stock
750g/1¹/₂ lb beef or veal tortellini
250g/8oz small peas
2 tablespoons chopped fresh tarragon
or 1 teaspoon dried tarragon

Onion confit
30g/1oz butter
2 onions, thinly sliced
2 teaspoons sugar
1 tablespoon chopped fresh thyme or
¹/₂ teaspoon dried thyme
1 cup/250mL/8fl oz red wine
2 tablespoons red wine vinegar

penne
with gorgonzola sauce

Method:

1 Cook pasta in boiling water in a large saucepan, following packet directions. Drain, set aside and keep warm.

2 To make sauce, place cream, stock, wine and Gorgonzola or blue cheese in a saucepan and cook, over a medium heat, stirring constantly, until smooth. Bring to a simmer and cook for 8 minutes or until sauce thickens.

3 Add parsley, nutmeg and black pepper (to taste) to sauce, bring to a simmer and cook for 2 minutes. Spoon sauce over hot pasta.

Serves 4

ingredients

500g/1 lb penne
<u>Gorgonzola sauce</u>
1 cup/250mL/8fl oz thickened double cream
1/2 cup/125mL/4fl oz vegetable stock
1/2 cup/125mL/4fl oz white wine
125g/4oz Gorgonzola or blue cheese, crumbled
2 tablespoons chopped flat-leaf parsley,
1/2 teaspoon ground nutmeg
freshly ground black pepper

pasta
with six-herb sauce

pasta with six-herb sauce

Serves 4

ingredients

500g/1 lb pasta shapes of your choice
<u>Six-herb sauce</u>
30g/1oz butter
2 tablespoons fresh rosemary, chopped
12 small fresh sage leaves
12 small fresh basil leaves
2 tablespoons fresh marjoram leaves
2 tablespoons fresh oregano leaves
2 tablespoons chopped fresh parsley
2 cloves garlic, chopped
¼ cup/60mL/2fl oz white wine
¼ cup/60mL/2fl oz vegetable stock

Method:

1 Cook pasta in boiling water in a large saucepan, following packet directions. Drain, set aside and keep warm.

2 To make sauce, melt butter in a saucepan over a medium heat. Add rosemary, sage, basil, marjoram, oregano, parsley and garlic and cook, stirring, for 1 minute.

3 Stir in wine and stock, bring to a simmer and cook for 4 minutes. To serve, spoon sauce over hot pasta and toss to combine.

types of pasta

Know your pasta

Angel-hair pasta: Also labelled as capelli di angelo, this is an extremely long thin pasta that is dried in coils to prevent it from breaking. Because of its delicate nature angel-hair pasta is best served with a light sauce.

Cannelloni: This large hollow pasta is most often stuffed, topped with a sauce and cheese, then baked. Cannelloni can also be stuffed and deep-fried until crisp.

If deep-frying, the tubes will need to be boiled before stuffing and frying. Lasagne sheets can also be used for baked cannelloni – spread the filling down the centre of the pasta then roll up.

Farfalle: Meaning 'butterflies', this bow-shaped pasta is ideal for serving with meat and vegetable sauces, as the sauce becomes trapped in the folds.

Fettuccine: A flat ribbon pasta that is used in a similar way to spaghetti. Often sold coiled in nests, fettuccine is particularly good with creamy sauces, which cling better than heavier sauces.

Lasagne: These flat sheets of pasta are most often layered with a meat, fish or vegetable sauce, topped with cheese, then baked to make a delicious and satisfying dish. Instant lasagne that you do not have to cook before using is also available.

Linguine: This long thin pasta looks somewhat like spaghetti but has square-cut ends. It can be used in the same way as spaghetti, fettuccine and tagliatelle.

Macaroni: Short-cut or 'elbow' macaroni, very common outside of Italy, is most often used in baked dishes and in the ever-popular macaroni cheese.

Orecchiette: Its name means 'little ears' and this is exactly what this pasta looks like. It is made without eggs and tends to have a chewier and firmer texture than some other pastas. Traditionally a homemade pasta, it can now be purchased dried from Italian food stores and some supermarkets.

Pappardelle: This very wide ribbon pasta was traditionally served with a sauce made of hare, herbs and wine, but today it is teamed with any rich sauce.

Penne: A short tubular pasta, similar to macaroni, but with ends cut at an angle rather than straight. It is particularly suited to being served with meat and heavier sauces, that catch in the hollows.

Shell pasta: Also called conchiglie, if large, or conchigliette, if smaller. The large shells are ideal for stuffing and a fish filling is often favoured because of the shape of the pasta. Small shells are popular in casseroles, soups and salads.

Spaghetti: Deriving its name from the Italian word spago meaning 'string', spaghetti is the most popular and best known of all pastas outside of Italy. It can be simply served with butter or oil and is good with almost any sauce.

Spiral pasta: Also called fusilli, this pasta is great served with substantial meat sauces, as the sauce becomes trapped in the coils or twists.

Tagliarini: Similar to fettuccine, this is the name often given to homemade fettuccine.

Tagliatelli: Another of the flat ribbon pastas, tagliatelle is eaten more in northern Italy than in the south and is used in the same ways as fettuccine.

Cooking pasta

Cook pasta in a large, deep saucepan of water: the general rule is 4 cups/1 litre/1¾pt water to 100g/3½oz pasta. Bring the water to a rolling boil, toss in salt to taste (in Italy, 1 tablespoon per every 100g/3½oz is usual), then stir in pasta. If you wish, add some oil. When the water comes back to the boil, begin timing. The pasta is done when it is 'al dente', that is tender but with resistance to the bite. Remove the pasta from the water by straining through a colander or lifting out of the saucepan with tongs or a fork.

You will find that the pasta quantities used in this book are fairly generous. In many cases, all you will need to make a complete meal is a tossed green or vegetable salad and some crusty bread or rolls.

Basic egg dough

1½ cups/185g/6oz plain flour
1 egg
1 teaspoon salt
1 tablespoon safflower oil

Method:

1. Mix flour and salt in a bowl until blended.
2. If using a food processor, process all ingredients for about 30 seconds. If the mixture forms a ball immediately and is wet to the touch, mix in flour by the tablespoon until the dough feels soft but not sticky.

   Note: If the mixture is too dry to work with, blend in water by the teaspoon until the dough just forms a ball.
3. If you have a pasta machine, the dough may be immediately kneaded and rolled out. If not using a pasta machine it may be better to wrap dough in plastic film and allow it to rest for about 15-30 minutes before rolling out.

Adjusting flour & liquid in dough

The moisture content of pasta dough is affected by a number of variables, including the type of wheat used, the age of the flour, its moisture content, and the degree of humidity in the air. For this reason, even when you measure the ingredients very carefully, you may need to adjust the proportions of flour and liquid if the dough seems too sticky or too dry to handle. Also, keep in mind that dough for filled pasta varieties will need to be more moist than dough for flat or tubular pasta. Add flour and water (no more than ½ teaspoon water or 1 tablespoon flour at a time as necessary, until the dough is the proper consistency for rolling, cutting or shaping.

Designer doughs

Using basic egg dough as a foundation, you can add different ingredients to create your own "designer" pastas with exciting colours and flavours. Experiment to your heart's content. Just remember that the colour and flavour of the pasta you make should compliment whatever sauce you plan to serve with it. Depending on which of the following ingredients you add, you may need to adjust the proportions of liquid and flour to form a dough of proper consistency.

- Puréed vegetables: cooked beetroot, roasted red, green or yellow capsicum (peppers), cooked pumpkin.
- Fresh puréed garlic
- Spices and seasonings: black pepper, cayenne, cinnamon, chilli powder, curry, nutmeg, saffron
- Fresh or dried black olives, finely chopped
- Fresh or canned hot chillies, finely chopped.

Making pasta by hand

Machines can be convenient for making pasta, but they are not essential. With only a bowl, a fork, and a rolling pin, you can turn out professional-quality fresh pasta in 10 minutes.

1 Make a ring of flour blended with salt on a clean work surface. Place beaten egg in centre of well. Use a fork or your fingertips to incorporate the flour into beaten egg so as to form a firm dough. On a flour-dusted work surface, knead dough until it is smooth and cohesive (5-8 minutes). Cover with a damp cloth for 15 minutes.

2 Lightly flour work surface. Begin with one third of the dough at a time. Starting from the centre and moving to the edge, roll the pasta using as few strokes as possible. If dough becomes too elastic, cover it for a few minutes with a damp cloth to prevent it from drying out. Roll out about .2 -.3cm ($^1/_8$ – $^1/_{16}$) in-thick.

3 Lightly flour dough and roll into a sponge-roll shape. Cut by hand to desired thickness for flat shapes (such as linguine, fettuccine, or lasagne). Dry 10-15 minutes on a pasta rack before cooking.

Making tortellini

Tortellini can be made with a variety of fillings, including the pumpkin filling shown here. Tortellini can be formed a few hours ahead and spread on lightly floured baking sheets. Make sure they do not touch. Cover and refrigerate or freeze before cooking. Follow directions for freezing as for ravioli.

1 The dough should be quite thin. Cut 5cm/2in) circles from dough. Put a scant teaspoon of filling in centre of each. Brush edges lightly with cold water.

2 Fold circle in half to enclose filling. Press edges firmly to seal.

3 With sealed edge out, place folded circle over index finger. Bring ends toward each other under the finger, turning sealed outer edge up to form a cuff. Pinch ends together firmly. Let dry for a few minutes on a lightly floured surface before cooking.

Preparing ravioli

Ravioli can be made with a variety of doughs and fillings.

Use the basic egg dough shown above, or your favourite flavoured dough recipe. The dough and filling should be compatible in flavour and colour.

The dough should be rolled quite thin. Using a mold to form the ravioli simplifies the process, but it is not essential. Ravioli can be prepared a few hours ahead of serving time and spread on lightly floured baking sheets. Make sure they do not touch.

Cover and refrigerate or freeze. Place in a lock-top plastic bag and use within 3 months. After cooking, ravioli can be added to broth or your favourite sauce.

Method for making ravioli:

1 *Roll pasta dough into thin sheets. Place mounds of filling, about ³/₄ teaspoon each, at regular intervals the length of the pasta. Brush lightly with cold water between the mounds.*

2 *Place another sheet of pasta over the first and use your fingers to press the sheets together between the mounds of filling.*

3 *Cut ravoli with a pizza cutter or pastry wheel. Use a fork to crimp and seal the edges.*

1

2

3

How much pasta to serve		
Pasta type	First course	Main Meal
Dried pasta	60-75g 2-2 ¹/₂ oz	75-100g 2 ¹/₂-3 ¹/₂ oz
Fresh pasta	75-100g 2 ¹/₂-3 ¹/₂ oz	125-155g 4-5 oz
Filled pasta	155-185g 5-6 oz	185-200g 6-6 ¹/₂ oz

weights & measures

Cooking is not an exact science: one does not require finely calibrated scales, pipettes and scientific equipment to cook, yet the conversion to metric measures in some countries and its interpretations must have intimidated many a good cook.

Weights are given in the recipes only for ingredients such as meats, fish, poultry and some vegetables, which is necessary for marketing, though a few grams or ounces one way or another will not affect the success of your dish.

Though recipes have been tested using the Australian Standard 250mL cup, 20mL tablespoon and 5mL teaspoon, they will work just as well with the US and Canadian 8fl oz cup, or the UK 300mL cup. We have used graduated cup measures in preference to tablespoon measures so that proportions are always the same. Where tablespoon measures have been given, these are not crucial measures, so using the smaller tablespoon of the US or UK will not affect the recipe's success. At least we all agree on the teaspoon size.

For breads, cakes, pastries, etc. the only area which might cause concern is where eggs are used, as proportions will then vary. If working with a 250mL or 300mL cup, use large eggs (60g or 2oz), adding a little more liquid to the recipe for 300mL cup measures if it seems necessary. Use the medium-sized eggs (55g or 1¼oz) with 8fl oz cup measure. A graduated set of measuring cups and spoons is recommended, the cups in particular for measuring dry ingredients. Remember to level such ingredients.

English measures

All measurements are similar to Australian with two exceptions: the English cup measures 10fl oz (300mL), whereas the Australian cup measure 8fl oz (250mL). The English tablespoon (the Australian dessertspoon) measures 14.8mL against the Australian tablespoon of 20mL.

American measures

The American reputed pint is 16fl oz, a quart is equal to 32fl oz and the American gallon, 128fl oz. The Imperial measurement is 20fl oz to the pint, 40 fl oz a quart and 160 fl oz one gallon. The American tablespoon is equal to 14.8mL, the teaspoon is 5mL. The cup measure is 8fl oz (250mL), the same as Australia.

Dry measures

All the measures are level, so when you have filled a cup or spoon, level it off with the edge of a knife. The scale below is the "cook's equivalent"; it is not an exact conversion of metric to Imperial measurement.

The exact metric equivalent is 2.2046 lb = 1kg or 1 lb = 0.45359kg

Metric	Imperial	
g = grams	oz = ounces	
kg = kilograms	lb = pound	
15g	½oz	
20g	⅔oz	
30g	1oz	
60g	2oz	
90g	3oz	
125g	4oz	¼ lb
155g	5oz	
185g	6oz	
220g	7oz	
250g	8oz	½ lb
280g	9oz	
315g	10oz	
345g	11oz	
375g	12oz	¾ lb
410g	13oz	
440g	14oz	
470g	15oz	
1000g 1kg	35.2oz	2.2 lb
1.5kg		3.3 lb

Oven temperatures

The Celsius temperatures given here are not exact; they have been rounded off and are given as a guide only. Follow the manufacturer's temperature guide, relating it to oven description given in the recipe. Remember, gas ovens are hottest at the top, electric ovens at the bottom and convection fan-forced ovens are usually even throughout. We include Regulo numbers for gas cookers which may assist. To convert °C to °F multiply °C by 9 and divide by 5 then add 32.

Oven temperatures

	C°	F°	Regulo
Very slow	120	250	1
Slow	150	300	2
Moderately slow	150	325	3
Moderate	180	350	4
Moderately hot	190-200	370-400	5-6
Hot	210-220	410-440	6-7
Very hot	230	450	8
Super hot	250-290	475-500	9-10

Cake dish sizes

Metric	Imperial
15cm	6in
18cm	7in
20cm	8in
23cm	9in

Loaf dish sizes

Metric	Imperial
23x12cm	9x5in
25x8cm	10x3in
28x 8cm	11x7in

Liquid measures

Metric	Imperial	Cup & Spoon
mL millilitres	fl oz fluid ounce	
5mL	1/6 fl oz	1 teaspoon
20mL	2/3 fl oz	1 tablespoon
30mL	1 fl oz	1 tablespoon plus 2 teaspoons
60mL	2 fl oz	1/4 cup
85mL	2 1/2 fl oz	1/3 cup
100mL	3 fl oz	3/8 cup
125mL	4 fl oz	1/2 cup
150mL	5 fl oz	1/4 pint, 1 gill
250mL	8 fl oz	1 cup
300mL	10 fl oz	1/2 pint
360mL	12 fl oz	1 1/2 cups
420mL	14 fl oz	1 3/4 cups
500mL	16 fl oz	2 cups
600mL	20 fl oz 1 pint,	2 1/2 cups
1 litre	35 fl oz 1 3/4 pints,	4 cups

Cup measurements

One cup is equal to the following weights.

	Metric	Imperial
Almonds, flaked	90g	3oz
Almonds, slivered, ground	125g	4oz
Almonds, kernel	155g	5oz
Apples, dried, chopped	125g	4oz
Apricots, dried, chopped	190g	6oz
Breadcrumbs, packet	125g	4oz
Breadcrumbs, soft	60g	2oz
Cheese, grated	125g	4oz
Choc Bits	155g	5oz
Coconut, desiccated	90g	3oz
Cornflakes	30g	1oz
Currants	155g	5oz
Flour	125g	4oz
Fruit, dried (mixed, sultanas etc)	185g	6oz
Ginger, crystallised, glace	250g	8oz
Honey, treacle, golden syrup	315g	10oz
Mixed peel	220g	7oz
Nuts, chopped	125g	4oz
Prunes, chopped	220g	7oz
Rice, cooked	155g	5oz
Rice, uncooked	220g	7oz
Rolled oats	90g	3oz
Sesame seeds	125g	4oz
Shortening (butter, margarine)	250g	8oz
Sugar, brown	155g	5oz
Sugar, granulated or caster	250g	8oz
Sugar, sifted icing	155g	5oz
Wheatgerm	60g	2oz

Length

Some of us are still having trouble converting imperial to metric. In this scale, measures have been rounded off to the easiest-to-use and most acceptable figures.
To obtain the exact metric equivalent in converting inches to centimetres, multiply inches by 2.54 Therefore, 1 inch equals 25.4 millimetres and 1 millimetre equals 0.03937 inches.

Metric	Imperial
mm = millimetres	in = inches
cm = centimetres	ft = feet
5mm, 0.5cm	1/4in
10mm, 1.0cm	1/2in
20mm, 2.0cm	3/4in
2.5cm	1in
5cm	2in
8cm	3in
10cm	4in
12cm	5in
15cm	6in
18cm	7in
20cm	8in
23cm	9in
25cm	10in
28cm	11in
30cm	1ft, 12in

index

Recipe	Page
Avocado salmon salad	44
Capellini with tomatoes	8
Caviar fettuccine	10
Cheesy meatballs and spaghetti	22
Chicken and leek rolls	14
Chicken and mango pasta salad	29
Chicken pasta salad	38
Chicken pasta toss	32
Chilli broad bean salad	63
Crests with mushrooms	66
Crispy noodles and vegetables	16
Fettuccine carbonara	23
Fettuccine pesto	58
Fettuccine with coriander sauce	11
Fettuccine with leeks	21
Fettuccine with spinach sauce	56
Fettuccine with corn sauce	65
Gnocchi with gorgonzola sauce	30
Grilled vegetable salad	68
Hot shallot and semi-dried tomato pasta	24
Linguine with chilli and lemon	56
Lobster in pasta nets	44
Macaroni with basil	62
Macaroni with tomato sauce	48
Minestrone	15
Noodles with bok choy sauce	16
Oriental vegetable noodles	50
Pasta shells with anchovy sauce	48
Pasta shapes with avocado sauce	28
Pasta with anchovies and basil sauce	51
Pasta with broccoli and anchovy sauce	45
Pasta with six-herb sauce	72

Recipe	Page
Penne bacon and basil	20
Penne napolitana	57
Penne with gorgonzola sauce	71
Penne with tuna, olives & artichokes	52
Pepperoni toss	33
Pork-and-sage filled ravioli	37
Quick fettuccine with scallops	46
Raspberry salmon pasta	43
Ravioli with lemon sauce	64
Ravioli with vegetable medley	20
Rigatoni with pumpkin	61
Scallop and capsicum pasta	42
Smoked chicken pappardelle	27
Spaghetti and pesto	13
Spaghetti basil soup	8
Spaghetti bolognaise	30
Spaghetti carbonara	35
Spaghetti with tuna and cress	42
Spirelli with ham	34
Tagliatelle with chilli octopus	47
techniques	76
Tomato and cheese lasagne	67
Tomato pasta rolls	12
Tortellini and avocado cream	60
Tortellini with onion confit	70
Traditional lasagne	26
Tuna-filled shells	53
Types of pasta	74
Vegetable and chilli pasta	59
Vegetable pasta salad	38
Warm pasta and salami salad	36
Weights & measures	78